The Cure

The Hero's Journey with Cancer

A Fable by G. Frank Lawlis, PhD

with Animal Illustrations by
Karen Emenhiser

Resource Publications, Inc.
San Jose, California

Editorial director: Kenneth Guentert
Managing editor: Elizabeth J. Asborno
Illustrations of immune system: Kathi Drolet

Reprint Department
Resource Publications, Inc.
160 E. Virginia Street #290
San Jose, CA 95112-5876

Library of Congress Cataloging in Publication Data
Lawlis, G. Frank.
    The cure : the hero's journey with cancer / a fable by G. Frank Lawlis.
        p.   cm.
    ISBN 0-89390-273-X
    1. Cancer—Psychological aspects. 2. Storytelling—Therapeutic use.
3. Imagery (Psychology) 4. Stress management. I. Title.
RC263.L358 1993 Suppl.
616.99'4'0019—dc20   93-29828

Printed in the United States of America

98 97 96 95 94 | 5 4 3 2 1

Contents

Preface

The human spirit has been an inspiration to me. The thousands of patients who have shared their pilgrimages into the challenge of life have been my teachers of courage and character. In my story of Alex, many stories are told, not only about the frustrations with the health professions and the confusing messages that get infused with the relationships, but also about the potential paths to health.

The Cure

Why is it that the worst news comes from the biggest people,
So that not only do we feel so bad, but also so weak and
  small?
It is like reliving the worst dream we had as a child,
Being brought before God and given a sentence with no
  recall.

One

The Diagnosis

"WHY DON'T YOU GO SEE A DOCTOR?" THE FALCON repeated in desperation. The falcon's friendship with Alex, the big gray wolf, spanned many years, almost since birth, and it frightened the falcon to see the big wolf in so much pain. "At least you would have some idea what you are dealing with. It is probably something about getting old or like an allergy."

"I know that you are probably right, but I keep thinking that I will get better, just as I always have done before," whispered Alex. Alex had learned to listen to the falcon's advice for many of his decisions. He first learned of the falcon's unique abilities to guide him on his hunting expositions and to help with responsibilities in caring for his large den. Later he found respect for his visionary leadership and economic choices. Yes, the falcon was a wise friend, and he knew that he would

eventually follow the falcon's recommendation, but he hated to go see the doctor for any reason. "I have had stomach aches before, and those were usually related to the food I ate, but this just hangs on and on. I have to admit I am not shaking it."

The falcon bristled when he felt the heavy fatigue and depression from his friend. Alex had always been one who never gave in to negative possibilities. When other wolves were starving and were afraid to venture out for fear that the hunters would shoot them, it was Alex who would lead the pack to food and new shelter. It was Alex's lack of fear and strong conviction that elevated the pack's respect for their leader. And now, the falcon heard another, albeit subtle, change in the big wolf's mood and self-confidence.

Alex slowly picked himself from the prone position of least pain and struggled to his feet. No movement was kind to him, and the effort to move any distance at all brought on a weakness and weariness deep in his belly. His movements were slow and deliberate as he made his way to the doctor's office.

The doctor's office was somewhat frightening to Alex, although he had been many times before, mostly for cuts and bites from hunting trips. He had consulted the doctor a few seasons ago when the pack had eaten poisoned meat. But this time was different. This time he sensed that the problem would not have a simple answer.

The doctor was a moody old bear, and if you caught him in a foul attitude, he could make you feel that it was a sin to get sick, or even worse to not get well quickly. He grunted and groaned as he went about his business with the single-mindedness of a detective investigating a crime. He exhibited little empathy for the patient; his focus was on diagnosis, the treatment, and the bill.

"Good morning, Alex. What brings you here again? Another patch-up job? You have more scars on you than you have skin," the bear addressed. He was in a good mood today, and Alex relaxed slightly.

"Well, Doctor, I have been having terrible pains in my stomach for several days. I can't eat much, and when I do, I throw all of it back up. I am weak all the time. I was hoping that you could fix me up with something."

The doctor looked concerned but went directly to work without much more than a frown. He mashed here, touched there, took some measurements, but Alex could not read much from his expressions. Time went on, but finally the bear said, "Alex, I don't know for sure, but I think we need to do some surgery. When we look inside, maybe we will know more."

The news was mystifying. Alex trusted the doc, and it was a bit comforting to at least have a plan. The exploration was scheduled immediately so that Alex would not have time to think too much about the surgery.

Alex awoke in the afternoon with a groggy head. He was aware of the doctor standing next to him, and of the doctor's anxiety, but he could barely understand much of anything else.

"It's cancer," said the bear. "I didn't try to cut it out because it would have done no good. I'm sorry. It's cancer and that is all I know."

Alex knew something about cancer from his experiences with other animals, so he tried to act rational. "What is cancer?" he asked, trying to clear his head of the nagging fog.

The bear seemed surprised and strained for an answer. "Well, it is like a growth, about the size of a frog in your belly, and it has spread, preventing your stomach from digesting your food. It is bad, very bad."

As Alex tried to process the information, the bear was anxious for permission to leave and took the silence as his opportunity. Alone, Alex tried to process this diagnosis. A frog, he thought, that was growing inside himself. How strange that this could happen. And why? Maybe he ate a frog egg, or maybe he didn't hear the doctor right. All his thoughts were dowsed with the heaviness of sleep and a fog of pain.

"Cancer!" The falcon's worse fears were realized. "What is cancer, other than a killer? What are you going to do?" questioned the falcon, trying to come to terms with his own fears more than actually listening to Alex. "And how is this devil frog going to kill you?"

Alex was lying with his head propped up, trying to be very still so that his stomach would hurt less. "All I know is what the doctor said. I went back to get a better idea of what I was dealing with, but he wouldn't sit still long enough to make any sense. I finally gave up and went home."

"What about your family? Do they understand it?" asked the falcon.

"My family is afraid of me. Perhaps they are afraid of catching it, but I really think they are afraid of my reactions. They have never seen me in this situation before, and they don't know how to respond if I begin to act differently than before."

"Your family loves you, but I understand their confusion as to how to help you if they were actually called for," the falcon proclaimed. "They don't want you to change from being the wolf you have always been."

For the first time in his life that he could remember, Alex felt totally isolated from everybody, even his good friend the falcon. Yes, he was loved, and his friend would listen, but they were all looking in, looking for support for their own fears. He looked at the falcon, wondering if he would still be a friend if everything changed.

As Alex appeared to gaze, the falcon grew more uncomfortable. "I think I will go do some errands," and off he flew with an unusual gracelessness.

Alex blamed himself for the departure of his friend. If he hadn't been so morbid or focused on his disease, he would be easier to be around. He had tried to direct his conversations away from the cancer, but the strain left a superficial overtone to the words. Either way, the uneasiness of relating had its impact upon all of the interpersonal transactions. His mate, his pups, his friends were separated from him in a way that he did not understand.

He was still confused about his lump that looked like a frog. He began to visualize a frog with a vicious face and sharp teeth eating away at his tissues. Alex began to eat large meals, believing that if he fed the monster in his gut, the monster would be too full to feed upon his body. The cancer began to develop a personality of its own. Some days it would be moody and cause pain with biting sensations throughout the body. Other days, it would be quiet, just lurking around. At night it would invade Alex's dreams with its presence.

"Alex," the falcon proclaimed one day, "you have gone too far within yourself. It may be true that no one else has this disease, but it seems to me that you have a choice. You can either give up and die quickly for the comfort for yourself and others, or you can fight the cancer. You know that I have always spoken my heart and you know that I love you. I will support you either way, but it would help me be with you and talk to you if I knew your direction."

The big wolf sighed with a heavy breath, "To tell the truth, I don't know my direction or path. It is like going to work when you expect to be fired. You want to quit and save the embarrassment of failure, end the frustration of being unable to satisfy the boss."

"Either way is a negative response," the falcon said with the softest response he could muster. "In your analogy with work, you are focusing upon the boss as someone who is against you, just as the cancer will defeat you. Go get another job; go see another doctor. All of your options are negative. Go see if there are any positive sides."

Alex smiled in his heart as he heard the falcon begin to repeat himself. Falcons had this habit of once they voiced their opinion they would begin to say it over and over again. It could become annoying, but Alex always thought it was funny.

Alex also knew that the falcon was right. He had taken one doctor's description and prognosis as the total truth, and this was completely against Alex's typical decision-making. Even in the hunts, Alex would allow even the youngest pup to give his opinions before a final direction was chosen. Yes, he would seek out other possible ideas on this cancer frog. After all, what did he have to lose?

Alex smiled at the falcon and said, "Let's go, my friend, and see what we can learn."

There is the sense that our disease is not a child-like thing,
But the result of some dark dungeon with the pot of seeds,
And the greatest conspiracy to our dreams and plans
Will be the downfall as the result of our most secret deeds.

Two

The Snake

IN SEARCH OF A DOCTOR WHO SPECIALIZED IN cancer care, the falcon located a snake who lived in an urban part of the forest and was noted for treating cases like Alex's. Although Alex had agreed to this venture, he was reluctant to go so far into such a highly populated area. Alex had always enjoyed the opportunity to roam in wide open areas, where he could escape his emotional problems from time to time. The doctor lived and worked in an area that afforded nothing but back-to-back patients. Alex had nothing against snakes except he had never understood them. To him, they always seemed to act as if they were a little better than other animals, a little arrogant maybe. But snakes were known as healers, so Alex finally arranged to make the trip.

The journey was hard on Alex. His body reminded him of each day of his life, and the cancer frog felt like an attacking shark every minute. It took three days to arrive at the thick bush where the doctor's office was, and he was so tired by the time he saw the doctor that Alex was wishing that the doctor would advise him to go home and die without having to do anything else. At least he could rest.

"Well Alex, I have heard a lot about you and I am glad to finally meet you," the doctor expressed at their first meeting.

Alex was taken back by this remark. He had never thought of himself as particularly noteworthy, and it made him curious. "What have you heard?" asked Alex with some concern that his condition might have been so bad that it had become news.

"Just that you are known as a fine hunter and rather clever in your exploits," smiled the snake.

The wolf realized and rediscovered a sense of the pride that had been absent for many days. "I have not been hunting for a long time, but with food so plentiful my lieutenants can handle the den needs now. Come this winter, I will have to start the old grind again. I hear the hunters will be out after our skins again."

The falcon had come with Alex and had been witnessing the dialogue from his perch. How impressed he was with this doctor. In a very subtle way, the doctor had accomplished two things in thirty seconds that the falcon had been trying to do for at least a moon. By this statement, the doctor had refocused Alex from identifying with his disease to being a hunter, and he had also determined whether or not Alex was expecting to be alive six months from now—the winter months.

The snake continued to ask perceptive questions about Alex's personal life, never inquiring directly as to the cancer impact. He asked about his family relationships, who his close friends were (this was also directed toward the falcon), and other health-related habits. All in all, it was a very pleasant experience. Tests and examinations occurred for almost two days, but there was always the hope that with this doctor's knowledge the cancer would be cured.

The second day the doctor laid out a treatment plan. "First, we are going to give you some strong medicine that may put your cancer into remission," explained the snake in a methodical tone. "The cancer is a tough one, and medicine may not work, but you can never tell if you are one of the lucky ones."

"What is cancer anyway, Doctor?" asked Alex without really understanding the treatment plan.

"Cancer? Well, cancer is like a bunch of ants gone crazy in your body. Your body is composed of cells, and for some reason, it has started producing these bad cells. And they are producing and going crazy like a bunch of ants on a hot day."

Alex was perplexed, straining to allow his mind to picture ants in his body. How did these ants relate to the frog? "How will the medicine help with the ants, or the cells?"

The snake coiled as high as he could in order to be authoritative and spoke in fast phrases, "I don't know what it will do to your cancer. Maybe it won't work at all."

"What I want to know is, if it did work, what would it do to the ants?" asked Alex, feeling that the dialogue was quickly being confused.

"What I said was that the cells, the cancer cells were like ants, not that they were ants!" the snake almost hissed in his declaration. "I recommend that you try the medicine to see if it works. After all, you might die without it."

16

Due to the doctor's apparent discomfort, Alex quickly softened his inquiry. "When do we get started, Doctor?"

"Today" was the single response of the doctor, and he slithered away to order the portions of medicine.

Alex and the falcon were quiet for a long time, even while the nurse administered the drug. Earlier they were so hopeful, but the last discussion undermined all belief in the doctor or his medicine. The falcon would not verbalize his rage at the snake and his lack of understanding about his friend's questions. Perhaps the greatest frustration was the sense in the beginning about the physician's apparent grasp of the situation. He began to wonder if it was his own interpretations of the interactions. Maybe it was just a structured interview they teach in medical school, and all the doctor was reciting was a list of questions from some other sensitive physician.

Alex directed his rage within himself. He felt foolish talking about ants. He surely was mistaken. He was glad he did not mention the frog to the doctor.

The drugs made Alex sicker than he had ever been. He lost all of his beautiful fur coat, down to his skins. Luckily the weather was warm; otherwise he would have been miserably cold. Not only was he uncomfortable from the physical elements but he had always taken a great deal of pride in his coat. The tattered appearance stripped whatever pride he had left after the nausea cut his energy low. He would hide from the world, fearing to venture out and meet someone. This was not the Alex whose courage was known throughout the area. This was not the Alex who knew himself first of all as a great wolf.

The falcon tried to convince Alex of the insignificance of his appearance, but he himself hardly recognized his old friend. Alex continued to lose weight, and with the loss of the fur and the deep depression reflected in the eyes, the falcon also began to lose hope. As this awareness arose in the consciousness of the falcon's mind, he grew uncomfortable and hated to face Alex with a depressed heart. It was torture to face his eyes, knowing the lies coming from his heart, as he tried to encourage the big wolf to face with dignity another day of weakness and loss.

"Alex, you appear to be gaining some weight," the falcon began a typical conversation. "I bet the medicine will take effect soon."

Alex looked into the falcon's eyes with a slow, desperate gaze. "I believe that I am going to die, and I do not want to die this way. I may live, but if I am going to live with a loss of dignity then this treatment may actually be worse than death!"

The falcon had heard these words before, but he had always convinced Alex to continue the treatment of the overall plan. But today there was a quiet resolve in his friend's voice. Although he would attempt to redirect his thinking, it was nice to hear that self-confidence again. "Oh Alex, you know you will do what the doctor says. It may take more time, and the disease—"

"What does the doctor know?" Alex remarked with more anger than before. "He talks as though I were a piece of meat. The other day I asked if there was some way that I wouldn't have to lose my fur, and you know what he said?"

Without stopping to hear the falcon's response, Alex went on. "He said that fur was not important. Everyone loses their hair anyway. Look at him! He has never had any hair." His voice was reaching a high pitch, almost like a growl. "I don't care what he says, I may be neurotic, but this treatment is taking away everything, my self-respect, my interest in life itself." All of a sudden Alex became very quiet.

These feelings came as no surprise to the falcon. When Alex had started the radiation treatments, and the scar tissue had thickened the sensitive belly skin, Alex had reacted with a disdain for the process rather than with hope. Alex was hating his cure. The doctor continued to focus upon the disease, insensitive to the great wolf's feelings. In fact, a battle of the wills evolved once the great hunter, now a patient, was expected to submit to the authority and demands of the medical profession.

The falcon attempted empathy. "I know that you are discouraged, but any day it may work—"

"This is not my expectation of life anymore," Alex interrupted again. "It is just not going to be my way of living or dying. I need to be more than a weak, naked, depressed bag of bones. If I can't trust my doctor to understand my needs for living with quality, I cannot expect him to understand my needs in dying with quality."

"Is it the doctor or the medicine, or the way you are reacting to the sickness?" asked the falcon after a long breath. "Because if it is the doctor, get another doctor. If it is the medicine, get some more medicine. But if it is the depression or nausea, you are just running away from it, and you are fooling yourself."

Alex thought for a long time, and finally responded, "I think you are right, and in my heart I don't think it is running away. I can handle whatever comes if I can face it with dignity. That's what I want most of all—dignity. That is much more important than life."

The falcon looked into Alex's eyes for the first time in months and said, "My friend, your dignity, your being, is the most important to me too." He knew that his friend's decision was made and unchangeable. But although the falcon was anxious about Alex's choice, he was relieved that he would not have to see the death of a soul as well as a body.

The snake was angry when Alex announced his decision to leave. He coiled and recoiled, hissing his prediction, "You will die; you will be sorry." But once he saw Alex's resolve, he quickly turned and slithered away.

Alex and the falcon wandered through the woods without communicating. Finally Alex sat down, and after a long breath, said, "Well, where do we go from here?"

"We find a path that will lead us to someone you can trust in," replied the falcon. "Let's find someone with a real interest in your inner self, or at least, whom you can relate to on a personal level."

Alex thought about this for a while and with a gleam in his eye said, "The minister, the owl, might be someone to talk to. He is a minister and should be able to understand the inner self."

"But does he understand cancer?" asked the falcon.

"The doctor did not understand about my soul, and nothing was worse than that. I will be able to deal with my frogs and ants if I know someone cares."

We all face fears and dreads, want to hide our desires and
     needs,
Yet, these are seen by heaven's judgment as faults and deeds.
Our secret urges might grow through the night to be the seeds
From which a disease will sprout and spread like devil's
     weeds.

Three

The Owl

THE OWL STARED AT THE WOLF AND HIS FEATHERED
friend with wide, encompassing eyes. Generally the owl
was considered to be a good preacher with good content
in his sermons, although no one could really say that
they knew him on a personal basis. The consensus was
that he led a private life, and everybody respected that.
As a him being a counselor, no one could or would say
that he or she ever went to the owl for help. Alex and
the falcon felt that it was worth at least a try, and they
approached him with respect and caution.

"Who-o are you?" the owl approached the pair directly.

"I am Alex," replied the wolf, also directly, "and this
is my friend. I have come to you for some consultation
about my physical condition, and my friend comes in
my support."

"I will help with God's guidance," the owl responded confidently.

"Do you know what cancer is?" asked Alex.

"Yes," replied the owl with a sense of clarity and definite authority. "I know what cancer is."

"Well, I have it, and the frog keeps biting me, and the ants keep running around in me, and—"

"My son," interrupted the minister in a very kind voice, almost like he was singing, "I know that you are frightened. I know that you have grave concerns about your life and your soul. Together we can deal with it."

Alex was perplexed by this response. The owl's eyes were wise and his voice sounded warm and caring, yet he did not understand the owl's words. Maybe the minister was trying to tell him something about the disease.

The falcon was equally confused. He had picked up on the minister's warmth and obvious support, but he was unsure about the words. What did he mean by "grave concerns about the soul"?

After a time of silence, Alex asked, "What exactly is cancer?"

"Before we answer that question, let us take a moment for prayer. Let us ask God to bless us and forgive us of our unfaithfulness," the minister said.

Alex and the falcon obediently bowed their heads. They respected the beliefs of many religions and had participated in many ceremonies. Alex had always felt that ritual brought him into a deeper sense of relaxation and serenity, and this felt right at this moment. He knew that much of his previous treatments were completely void of anything except physical attention. Spiritual attention offered a hope that he would begin to feel better at some level.

After the prayer, Alex asked again, "Minister, what is cancer?"

"My son," the owl began with a slow pace, "cancer is sin. It is sin against the body, the mind, and the spirit. If you are to live, then you must repent to the Lord."

Alex was surprised by the accusation of the minister. Sure, he had done some things he was not proud of, even some things wrong, but the direct assumption that he was being punished defensively for his actions left him without a response.

"My son," the minister interrupted his thoughts. "Do you repent for your sins?"

"I have repented of my sins for a long time. For every wrong act committed, I have always tried to make it right. I have repaid my debts, and I have taken care of my friends. I do not pretend to be perfect and there are many ways I could do better, but I do not understand what I am repenting for."

"Pride, lust, selfishness!" exclaimed the owl. "Can you tell me you have not experienced these?"

Alex thought for a moment, "Yes, I admit that I have had these thoughts arise, but doesn't everyone?"

"It says in the Bible, 'Whatever exists in the mind is the same as committing the act,' and you are guilty for all you do," pronounced the minister.

Alex and the falcon looked at each other with similar thoughts. Finally the falcon said contemplatively, "Perhaps the thoughts are merely temptation to us rather than actual intention. I have had lustful, prideful and selfish thoughts, but thoughts can be reconsidered. That is the wonderful thing about my dreams and images. I can rehearse them over and over again and play them with different endings. I can learn from the dreams and thoughts without carrying them out."

Alex reflected, "I can see the difference between a thought that is continuously lustful or vindictive and that dwells until it blinds you with a negative perspective and a thought that is constructive in dealing with lustful and vindictive issues."

"It says in the Bible, 'Whatever—'" the minister attempted to break in the conversation, but Alex and the falcon were heavily invested in their discussion of thoughts.

"It would be very sad if we could not think through our problems, even though they had destructive qualities to them. If people did not have the ability to process their negative feelings this way, how would they resolve their feelings?" asked the falcon.

"It says in the Bible—" the owl continued but was drowned out by Alex's remarks.

"They would have to play out in real life. In fact, one can predict the adjustment of a youngster, based on whether or not the cub can imagine an event's outcome, as well as predict the consequences of behavior."

"What happens to those who can't express their feelings and imagine the outcomes if they were to act on them? " asked the falcon.

"Some turn out to be criminals. Some just create problems that interfere with hunting expeditions and with getting along with the pack. We try to train these pups with specific rules, since they are handicapped by lack of imagination," the big wolf replied.

Finally they refocused their attention on the owl. Alex addressed him with another leading question. "If thoughts are used as learning experiences, would you consider such thoughts a sin?"

The minister skirted the question. "Do you believe you have never made a mistake or committed a sin? Because if you think that, you are wrong, and you are committing a sin with your pride and deceit."

Alex sat back and took a long, deep breath. "It seems to me that all of us commit sins, or at least we think we do, and certainly we all make mistakes. I know of no perfect animal who never screwed up at some time. As pups we are taught that we make mistakes, and we probably never forget that message."

"Do you thank you are better than other animals? You don't appear to have the ability to understand sin as the rest of us," responded the owl, sneering sarcasm.

"To answer the question you asked, no, I don't think I am better than other animals. But you may be right about your assumption. I have not been blessed with a lot of guilt, because that seems to be what you are talking about. Guilt is the part of the brain that tells you that you should feel pain, for the sake of pain, for all your mistakes of a lifetime. Every time you make a new mistake and have an accident, all of the old pain is added to the new stuff," Alex said as if he was talking to his pups.

Alex continued, "Guilt has been associated with being necessary for learning, like having to feel some pain in order to remember not to hit others or steal from others. But that is *responsibility*, not guilt. Besides, Minister, I was taught that forgiveness and love were the main messages of the Bible."

The owl did not answer. He rearranged himself in his nest and said, "We should pray. Please bow your heads and I will ask the Lord to help you."

Alex and the falcon bowed their heads, but their minds were still restless with the issues of sin. Alex kept thinking: If cancer is sin, and sin is thinking about guilt, and I have very little investment in guilt, then why do I have the cancer?

The minister began his prayer, "God, forgive us of our sins, for we have committed great sins today and yesterday. Heal us of our self-centeredness, of our pious attitudes, of our lustful thoughts for our neighbors. We are not worthy of your love. We are not worthy in your sight. We ask your blessings."

The falcon was the first to leave. Alex walked out slowly, with his head down. The falcon thought at first that the great wolf was depressed, but he soon realized that he was thinking very intently.

After they had gone some distance, Alex finally broke the silence. "There *is* a difference between spirituality and religion, don't you think?"

"Well, I have known some spiritual folks who were not religious in a church doctrine thing," answered the falcon. "And I have known some religious people who were not spiritual in a philosophical way. Yes, I would agree that I see a difference."

Alex thought a while longer and said, "I am afraid that the owl's god is not my God. My God would have never wanted me to pray like that. My God is loving and caring, not hateful and harmful. No, the way to my spiritual path is not through the owl's religion."

Alex put his head down and became very quiet. The falcon felt his friend's loneliness, even in his company. The awareness of another separateness was heavy. Through the efforts to deal with his disease, Alex had faced the separation from his family, his religion and perhaps his community as well. He was weighing his whole belief system and its validity against the challenge of the frogs, ants and sin of cancer.

The mind used to be simple, telling us how to get here or
    there,
Telling our bodies what to eat, when to run, what to see,
Until Dr. Freud revealed that within us all lies a monster,
And if suppressed, one day a tumor may grow to be.

Four

The Eagle

ALEX WAS DEPRESSED. THE DREADFUL FROG IN HIS
gut had begun to eat away at his life. The ants were
swarming, producing a nausea in his head that left his
mind disoriented. He began to forget things easily. He
stumbled over his words and thoughts. He could see the
kind forgiveness in the eyes of his family and friends as
he attempted to express his feelings regarding a decision
of the pack. He began to doubt his own abilities.

The falcon also began to doubt Alex's mental
capacities. There was no joy or excitement in their
companionship, only a heavy feeling of sorrow. In fact,
an unconscious agreement existed between them that
said the falcon would not expect from Alex anything
physical or mental. There had been too many great
moments wherein the wolf had demonstrated cunning
and wisdom in pack decisions as well as in the hunt,

but the present moments of forgetfulness and confusion were too embarrassing for those who respected him. The pups giggled at his struggles for self-composure, and the elders turned their heads. Alex had numbed himself by internalizing, as if he was carrying on a conversation with himself and no one else was around. In fact, he would begin to speak out loud with no one listening. His bizarre behaviors made everyone, including the falcon, afraid of what might happen next.

One day the falcon finally had enough of the frustration and blurted out, "Alex, you are depressed and getting worse! If you don't care anymore about your life, you can blow me off, but your attitude is ruining all your relationships. I am going to take you to a shrink, a psychiatrist."

Alex focused upon his falcon friend, who was only a few inches away from his nose. "A psychiatrist? Why? What can he do? Can he get rid of the frog? The ants? The sin? He would deem me crazy."

"Well," retorted the falcon, "maybe so, but you have to do something. You are driving everyone who cares for you crazy."

The psychiatrist, an eagle, pierced Alex's consciousness as they entered the office. He said nothing but looked fiercely at the pair, analyzing each movement. He waited for either Alex or the falcon to speak.

"We are here to help my friend, Alex," announced the falcon after a seemingly eternal period of silence.

"Then what are you doing here?" addressed the eagle to the falcon.

"Only here as a friend," said the falcon. The meetings of falcons and eagles are always a bit tense anyway, and the falcon was more than uncomfortable.

"Then leave. Alex has to learn to deal with his problems himself," the eagle instructed in a brisk manner.

Obediently the falcon left with some feeling of relief. He did not like the constant stare of the eagle nor his abrupt approach. The falcon now had his doubts about the wisdom of bringing his friend to such a place, but he reconciled himself with the reason that something was better than nothing.

Alex was afraid, but in his characteristic way, he would not show it. He sat himself in the place designated by the eagle and waited for the next move. He reminded himself to breathe slowly, using his keen sense of smell to familiarize himself with the environment. He did note a wide variety of emotional overtones, but nothing specific came to mind. He began to survey the personal artifacts in the psychiatrist's setting in hopes of understanding the eagle's mind. After all, this psychiatrist was going to try to read his mind, so a little information might help defend himself.

"You seem to be very resistant to revealing yourself," reflected the psychiatrist, breaking Alex's train of thought.

"Yes, uh, no, I was just waiting to see what was supposed to happen. I have never been to a shrink, uh, a psychiatrist before," responded Alex somewhat defensively.

"No, you are trying to out-guess what I am going to do to your mind, aren't you?" confronted the eagle.

Alex felt embarrassed by the eagle's direct question as well as by the correctness of the declaration. "Yes, I have some concern about my problems, but I really don't know how to relate them to you, a stranger. I know that you are an expert in these things, but usually I take my concerns to someone I know and trust. I don't know how to find immediate ease."

"What you're really trying to say is that you want a father figure so that you can feel nurtured," said the psychiatrist, as if he were programmed to respond in so many words and with so much emotion.

Alex thought about this for a moment, "I suppose my grandfather might have been someone to whom I could talk, but my father would not be someone like that."

"A-ha!" exclaimed the eagle. "You are dealing with some old expectations of your father. You have been depressed by your failures, and now you are feeling the anxieties and guilts."

Again Alex pondered the interpretations of the psychiatrist but finally responded slowly, deliberation integrated with each word, "Actually I have come to you because I have cancer, something like an angry, sinful frog or angry ants, and my family and friends are beginning to worry about me. To tell the truth, I do not like anything anymore. I am a being who likes to take a lot of pride in myself, yet I have let myself go. I don't get up in the mornings with any hopes of achieving anything. I lost a lot of my fur that I used to be very proud of. It's growing back, but the dignity hasn't. What can you tell me to care anymore?"

The psychiatrist just looked at him with eagle-hard eyes and nodded as if Alex had not completed his sentence.

The great wolf slumped then almost fell into a curled knot, crying. He whined and howled without actually saying a word for almost half a day. When he looked up, the eagle had flown away. He must have had other things to do and had probably returned, but once he had seen that Alex would be going through his crying spell for some time, he had just left. Anyway, that is the way Alex figured it out. Alex was exhausted from his experience. He had finally released months of grief and felt some relief, but he was tired. The great wolf closed his eyes and fell into a deep sleep.

It was one of the first restful sleep periods he had had in a long time, and he dreamed long continuous scenes. He dreamed of many hunts and good times with his family and his friends. One dream he would remember when he awoke was about being in a large meadow, probably around the middle of spring because the trees were in full leaf, the aroma of the flowers was pervasive and the sun rays were warm. He cold feel the softness of the earth beneath his paws as he ran through the meadow. He was aware of a brisk nip in the new morning air, although he did not feel any of the usual ache in his joints on such mornings as these.

As he slowed to a walk, he saw a body of water, like a pond or small lake, surrounded by large rocks. As he neared the rocks he could make out a figure of another wolf, like him except that the other wolf was much larger. He was frightened at first but continued to walk toward this figure, attempting to sense out this interesting entity. When he was about two wolf lengths away from the creature, he stopped with a breath. This was no wolf. It had some general characteristics of a wolf—a nose, a forehead—but it looked different this close. His eyes looked straight at Alex. It was not a fearful look but one of understanding and wisdom.

"Alex?" it asked. "Alex, is that you? I have been waiting for you, but I am not sure it is you."

Alex was surprised that this creature knew his name but stumbled through a response. "Yes, I am Alex. But since you knew my name, why didn't recognize me?"

"Recognize you?" replied the creature. "Alex, you have to remember that you are many things, and anybody could be confused by your shape or form."

"I don't understand," said Alex. "I have always had the same coat of fur since I was a pup. Although my body has some more fat than it had when I was younger, I look basically the same as I usually do. By the way, how do you know me, and who are you?"

"I am J., and we have known each other for many years," answered the creature. "And under different situations. You, too, have changed. Look at your paws."

Alex did not understand but looked at his paws anyway. What had been paws were now claws. He quickly looked at his fur, which was not longer the lovely coat, but feathers. He was a bird! He looked with questioning eyes at J., the creature, as if to ask for the meaningfulness of this transformation.

Finally he spurted words out, although they were hard to express with a bird's communication system. "What happened? I am a wolf! I have been a wolf, and that is all I know about being. How can I be a bird?"

37

"You are much too hard on yourself, Alex," responded J. "You are many things that were and should be. Look at yourself now."

Alex was almost too afraid to look again, and the surprise was just as difficult to comprehend even with the preparation. His claws were now fins and his feathers were a skin of scales. He was a fish. His mind swam for understanding and order.

J. interrupted his thoughts, "Alex, you were many things, and you will be many things, but you will always be you. See yourself as you are, not as your ego or limited nature sees you."

Alex looked down at himself again, but recognized no form, no hair, no scales, nothing but a slimy transparent ooze. In this form, he could not make any communication with the creature, but the creature knew his thoughts. He wondered if this was the way of death and if he was dying.

"No," the creature answered. "This is the way of life, and you are to love yourself for what you are. This is a gift."

Alex awoke from his slumber with a jerk. The dream was over. He quickly examined himself. Yes, he was a wolf again. He kept reminding himself over and over again that it was a dream, only a dream.

Suddenly he remembered he was at the psychiatrist's office, and he looked up to find the eagle in his usual place, observing Alex's behavior.

This time the eagle spoke first. "You slept and had dreams. Tell me if you can remember them."

Alex cleared his head. "I must have been more exhausted than I realized." The great wolf wrestled with his thoughts but finally said, "I did not know that I was so depressed. I cried for a long time. It was horrible to cry that way, but I feel better to finally let it out. I do feel better than I have in a long time."

"Your dreams. Can you remember your dreams?" inquired the psychiatrist.

"Yes, I was coming to that," said Alex. "None of this really makes any sense, but if you want to know, I'll report what I saw."

Alex described his last dream in as much detail as possible. The eagle listened very intently to the detailed dream but did not ask much about the creature named J.

After a long pause at the end of the dream, the eagle finally spoke, "You know, of course, that the cancer could very well be a manifestation of the psychiatric conflict related to the fixation complex between you and your mother. That is, by keeping the sexual impulses hidden far down in your subconsciousness, sooner or later it would be expressed by disease."

Alex did not understand. "Are you saying that the cancer had something to do with my mother?"

"The cancer is in your stomach, a normal region associated with the womb," explained the psychiatrist. "As you have been attempting all your life to replace your father for the attentions of your mother, the libidinal energy has been focused upon this area, making it extremely vulnerable to disease."

"But my father died before I was born."

The eagle was silent for some time, then said, "You appear to be resisting the point of the analysis. Your mother probably wanted you to substitute for your father, but you are incapable of performing at one function or another. At any rate, you have felt inadequate all of your life, and now the inadequacy is expressing itself through your cancer."

Alex pondered this possibility and inquired, "Did the dream tell you this, Doctor?"

"The dream is a vehicle for unconscious material, Alex. The 'creature' in your dream was your mother expressing her dissatisfaction with you. The forms of a bird, a fish and a uni-cellular structure were expressions of sexual forces. The bird related to sexual energy. The fish obviously relates to the snake, a major symbol of sexuality, and the uni-cellular form is the embryonic stage of new life, the by-product of sexual relations," concluded the eagle with a self-satisfied huff.

Alex was confused and perplexed. Rather than continuing on with more confusion, he excused himself from the presence of the psychiatrist and went back into the woods. The eagle was eager to pursue more dreams and analysis but was not insistent. He gave another appointment time before concluding the session.

"How did it go?" asked the falcon after Alex had gone into the forest several steps. He whispered his question although there was no need.

Alex found a comfortable and private place for him and his friend to discuss the meeting. At last he said, "I found out some very important things in there. First, I discovered how depressed I was, and how much I was holding in myself. I finally broke down and cried. I really let it out."

The falcon was surprised by this admission since he had so rarely seen his friend ever admit to sad feelings. He was a little hurt that he had been left out of such an intimate moment. "Did he make you cry or tell you to cry? Why did you let it out with him, and not with your friends?"

Alex felt the hurt of rejection in his friend's voice. "No, it had very little to do with the doctor. It was more of a situation where it was just O.K. In fact, the eagle left for most of the time while I wept and slept."

The falcon reflected upon Alex's words. He found himself feeling uncomfortable as he listened to his friend's words about his behavior—behavior that was so out of character for the big wolf. It was difficult to imagine Alex acting as he described.

"The second thing I learned," Alex continued, "was the strange way psychiatrists interpret dreams and your problems. I told him about a dream I had, and he told me that it told him my cancer was all involved with me and my mother, being involved with sexual things. He may be right because he is the expert on this stuff, but it doesn't feel right."

"My friend," the falcon said, "the mind works in mysterious ways, and I can see a difference in you. I think that you should try it a little longer for your mental health."

Alex did return to the psychiatrist several times, but he found it difficult to understand the interpretations. He did benefit from the freedom to explore his feelings, and his depressions were more interesting to talk about, but he felt that the discussions were going in circles. Finally one day, Alex said to the falcon, "I have been thinking about the conclusions of the psychiatrist. If I accept them as totally valid and true, what could I do now? If I did have this neurotic need for my mother to accept me as my father, and if I do have all of this turmoil in my stomach because of that, what could I do now? Should I demand this role with my mother, or what?"

The falcon was hoping Alex would not expect an answer. He knew that this was a psychiatric question, not one for discussion with a friend who knew nothing about psychiatry. Finally, he said, "I do not know, but I cannot see where you are going with this."

"Well, where I am going is in circles," proclaimed the great wolf. "It seems to me that my neurosis is just as incurable as my cancer. What I have now are two diseases instead of one, and I am supposed to feel better about it than before. I need to find someone who will stop diagnosing me so well and begin to help me get rid of it. So far I have been diagnosed with a mad frog, crazy ants, sin and a severe hang-up with my mother."

The falcon looked Alex straight in the eye. "My friend, we will fight on until we do all that we can."

And they left to find another way.

We grow up with certain ideas about our health,
Seeing illness as an army of germs or a product of the food
   we eat.
Could illness possibly be the tricks and antics of heaven,
Challenging us to fight to success or defeat?

Five

The Bull

EARLY ONE MORNING, THE FALCON CAME FLYING TO
Alex as fast as he could. He was talking so fast that Alex
was having difficulty understanding what he was saying.

"Alex! Alex! I have great news! There is a special
doctor on the other side of the woods, close to the lake,
who has cured cancer. He is a bull, and he believes that
exercises are extremely powerful for cancer cure."

Alex had been feeling pretty optimistic about himself
and was eager for a walk. He greeted his friend without
much regard for his news but primarily for his
enthusiasm. Without question as to the validity of the
bull's credentials or methods, they immediately set out
for the trip. The summer had done its part in helping
Alex regain most if his silky fur, and Alex felt lighter
and slimmer. Taking his own stride, the great wolf could
keep pace for about half of his normal distance. He

would have to rest periodically. The falcon was patient with his friend's slower pace.

Toward the end of the day, they arrived at the edge of the pasture where the bull resided. They looked about but did not find him at his usual place. Rather than continue the search, Alex decided to spend the night and find the bull the next day. He located a safe, cool spot under a tree trunk and quickly fell asleep.

Alex had many dreams that night. He also dreamed about the wise creature, J., again, only this time he got to ask the questions. This time, he approached J. as an old friend, with no fear.

"J., although I do not recognize you, I do feel as if I have known you before. Where have we met?"

The creature gazed into the sky and said, "At one time I was among many who were starving, and you came to us and helped us. At another time I was cold, and you gave me shelter. I came to see you for advice, and you gave me love and guidance."

Alex was aware that he had been helpful to the other animals in the forest from time to time, but he had not thought that much about it. However, he did not remember helping out anyone like this creature.

The creature continued, "Remember, you are you, and I am I. We are what we become. I am not what you remember because I have taken another form, but nothing changes. Nothing changes."

Just as Alex began his bodily transformations, as before, he awoke.

The falcon had found the bull and had awakened Alex for a consultation. Alex gradually got up from his resting place, still remembering the dream and also moving his joints to clear the tightness from his muscles. After he had regained better focus for the day, he moved in the direction of the bull.

The bull was a very large type with tremendous muscle development in his shoulders. His voice, with a booming loudness in each word, hurt Alex's sensitive ears. The bull paced as he talked, like a coach talking to a team, not directing his speech to anyone in particular. In fact, it was always difficult to tell if the doctor was looking directly at anything. One of his eyes tended to be disconnected from the other, moving in different directions. Alex did not know which one to concentrate on, and it became a internal guessing game as to what the bull might be addressing. Later Alex and the falcon would have many laughs about this strange habit.

In a gruff voice the bull addressed Alex, "Boy, you look puny. I can see right now that we have a lot of training ahead. Yes, I think that a program of physical fitness will do a world of good."

Although these words were said in an enthusiastic and positive way, Alex felt a wave of depression hit him. After all, he had had a good body most of his life, and what this doctor was saying was that he was unpleasant to look at.

Defensively, Alex tried to explain his physical status. "I have been sick lately, and a lot of my muscles have been weak so that I have not been getting as much exercise as usual."

"Sickness is a form of attitude," retorted the bull. "We tend to baby ourselves at the least thing. I can remember going to work many a day with a high fever and diarrhea, but I used my mind to control my body. That's the main thing to know, mind over matter."

Alex had an image of how the doctor's patients and staff reacted to the situation described by the bull, and he smiled to himself but maintained his line of thought. "Can you help me with my cancer?"

"Cancer!" exclaimed the bull. "I have helped many people with cancer. As I have said before, mind over matter works for everything. Look at me. I work out all day, everyday, and I am as fit as a fiddle."

"Have you had cancer?" asked the wolf.

"No, I have always kept myself in shape and perfect health, working out all day everyday."

Alex was beginning to feel like he was dealing with the owl and his sense of sin, only this time it was the sin of getting unhealthy. Because the bull was using

himself so much as the ideal, Alex began to question the doctor's lifestyle further.

"What do you do when there is work to be done, like food gathering and den clearing?"

"Oh, I never have to do those kinds of things. My food is given to me or I just roam. My only work is to keep my girls happy, if you know what I mean," replied the bull.

Alex fell into a long silence as he tried to figure out what relevance all this had to do with his disease. Yes, he was out of shape, and he had enjoyed exercise, especially games. He did not know if he could manage exercising all day, but he would give it a try.

Obediently he began the exercise routine, at least to the best that he could. Day after day he would attempt to keep up with the rest of his group, but he would become exhausted in the middle of the program. Although he was the oldest by many years, his pride would not allow any slack in performance.

After three weeks of the conditioning, Alex did admit to thinking better and feeling less depressed. He had begun a strong dislike for the exercise, although there was a strong association between his feeling about the exercise and the snobbery of the exercise crowd itself. Their fundamental principle was that no one should admit to sickness, and therefore, it would not exist. Alex had to admit that he did not see anyone who got sick, but people would leave. Maybe it was a selection process for only the strong, those with excellent genetic backgrounds or with neurotic needs for this philosophy, or maybe it was just youth.

Alex was sick, and although his condition did stabilize somewhat, the bull became more frustrated with his lack of progress. After many days of intense attention, Alex felt the bull's loss of interest. In fact, there was a subtle feeling of embarrassment about Alex's presence, as if he represented a failure to the system. Probably more from this persistent message than a from a personal lack of success, Alex left the program.

"Did you feel that it might have worked if the bull had had a different personality?" asked the falcon.

Alex pondered and finally said, "The doctor was both a problem and a solution. He represented success, and I yearned for success to the point that I could taste it. He represented renewed youth and vitality. But at the same time, his path was not mine. If only he could have looked at me for who I am instead of as a reflection of himself, we may have made more headway."

The falcon was still puzzled. "Do you think that the exercise made a difference? Are you going to keep at it?" The falcon was thinking about his friend returning to the downward spiral he had witnessed before.

"Yes, yes, I think that I began to feel the rhythm of life within myself. At least, I can feel the life force. When pushed to the brink of physical strength, you begin to know there is something there."

With a satisfaction in his voice, the falcon said, "I must admit that I am relieved to hear that. I have another doctor for you to see."

Alex looked at his friend with a disgruntled frown. "Don't you get tired of finding all of these doctors? I am getting pretty tired of being the test case for all of these methods."

"You can't stop looking," the falcon said with a commanding voice. "The fact that there are so many treatments out there indicates that there are many ways of dealing with cancer, and one of them may be the way for you."

Alex was not surprised at the falcon's words. He knew that his friend was experiencing fear and frustration at seeing this disease take its toll. He recognized that the falcon's role as friend was quickly becoming that of caretaker. He had a deep-seated feeling that if he allowed that role to emerge, the falcon might cease to be a supportive confidant—maybe even become part of the ongoing problem by making demands for finding a cure. Alex needed room to make his own decisions, not to be rescued.

Alex smiled. "It may also indicate that there is no one way, just a lot of people trying to be the first to solve the problem, and it's all up for grabs since there is no definite answer anyway."

A chill went down the falcon's spine. He was afraid that Alex had heard his own fears, and the thought of his friend's loss of hope would be the end. He looked down at the ground, hoping that Alex would not see the fear in his eyes. He was searching for a response when Alex interrupted his thought process.

"Don't look so disturbed, my friend. I have learned a lot on this journey. I may have lost the expectation of finding a cure, but now I am curious about what the next healer will say. Tell me what you have found."

Alex had felt the falcon's depression and knew that he should be more protective of his friend's efforts. Out of his concern for the falcon's feelings and hopes, he mustered up the enthusiasm for another visit. He was not clear about this path, but at least it was better than nothing, and if it made his friend feel less afraid to see him do something, then why not?

However, Alex did make a mental note that he might have to establish a boundary between him and the falcon about responsibility and cheerleading. It was sad to think that the love between the two friends might actually create some separation and confusion. For now, it was their fear and anxiety speaking, and that was forgivable. But a discussion would be in order if he began to allow his friend to take over his life—or death—process.

"You are what you eat" they say, considering what is
    nutritious.
The human being can process almost anything with ease.
"Food" is just another word for "energy." The stuff of life,
Like poor fuel in a sports car, can turn into disease.

Six

The Deer

THE DEER'S EYES WERE SOFT AS THEY GAZED AT ALEX, and the great wolf felt uncomfortable with their seductiveness. For many years, he had known this nutritional healer as a committee member in the forest meetings, and Alex had a great deal of respect for the deer's intuitions. Soft-spoken and gentle, the deer had a reputation for being firm about his rights without being hostile. In fact, many of the individuals who knew the deer felt that he could hypnotize them with his eyes, and he could will them to do what he wanted. Now, Alex understood what they were talking about.

"Doctor," Alex began, "I have a disease called cancer, and I am told that you know what I can do to cure it. Can you help me?"

"It depends," responded the deer. "It depends upon your willingness to do what I will tell you to do."

Alex glanced at the falcon with a suspicious eye. "What exactly would you want me to do?"

"I want you to read and educate yourself on everything I tell you. There will be much for you to learn about how to make yourself well. You will need to spend many hours reading books."

Alex thought for a moment, then asked, "Will you explain to me what cancer is? I have been told it is a frog that eats your guts, a bed of ants with stinging bites,

a sin against God, a neurotic relationship with my mother, and a case of poor physical conditioning. I am confused."

"You are confused because all of those doctors try to cure you through the mistaken idea that cancer is based upon something gone wrong in the body. They persistently look for something that is in error. There is nothing wrong with you. You are perfectly healthy."

Alex was really confused with this information. Slowly he brought together the words for the obvious question. "Why do I feel the way I do, sick all the time?"

The deer was waiting for just such a question and in a self-satisfied, almost gloating manner of speech, he said, "It is the world that is sick. Just think, what do you put into your body for fuel, fuel to move, fuel to think, fuel to live?" Without giving Alex time to respond, he went on, "Food! Food! Food is what we take in for our subsistence. What else? Air! Of course, air is necessary for our moment-to-moment existence. And what else? Water? Yes, water is extremely critical to our health. Don't you see? Food, air, and water are the critical elements for health, and without them we have disease."

Alex had been watching the deer's eyes all this time, and he was having trouble catching the logic of the doctor. His head was swimming and he really did not want to think. Automatically he nodded his head in agreement.

The doctor went on, "What happens when the food, air and water are unhealthy? I will tell you what happens. It makes you unhealthy. It only stands to reason that if you take in unhealthy things, you eventually become what you eat—unhealthy. Do you see what I mean?"

Alex nodded, but he was having more and more difficulty concentrating. The doctor could have said anything and Alex would have agreed. Perhaps this was the plan, to mesmerize Alex into a feeling of well-being so that the pain would go away.

The deer gave Alex a number of books and articles on the evils of food and environment contamination, with the promise that on the next visit the specifics would be memorized. Loaded down with the materials, Alex found a place for study and proceeded to conquer the information. Alex learned that sugar and salt were bad for the harmonic balance and probably major causes of depression and high blood pressure. There were studies relating the dangers of meat, lettuce, nuts, chicken, and several versions of fish. Any type of meat or dairy product was absolutely connected to disease of one form or another. To make things even more complicated, even if a food was approved, it was probably contaminated in the way it was processed and not recommended for consumption. For example, milk was probably processed from an animal that was doctored with antibiotics, creating a vulnerability to yeast growth. Any type of vitamin supplementation may or may not be helpful, depending upon one's own need for vitamins. Sugar and salt were typically added for taste and preservative reasons, making it as unhealthy as anything else.

The contamination of the air and water was not new to Alex. He had tasted the differences since the mills were built a few years ago. Fish had begun to die and wash up on the banks of his favorite drinking places. He was left with the conclusion: He had to protect himself from his own world.

"How astute your observations," noted the deer at their next meeting. "We must protect ourselves from all the dangers that await us and be aware of the death that surrounds us." As he spoke, his eyes glistened and his mouth watered as if he were relishing the thoughts of exposing boogiemen from their hiding places. The deer looked from side to side, speaking in a low voice, as if he held a secret from the forest.

Alex was intrigued for a period, primarily because of the hypnotic manner of the deer, and partly because he felt like he belonged to a select group of animals knowledgeable to the secrets of poison. He went into the formal process of training to learn how to prepare food for appropriate health care.

The lessons were complicated and strict. Things could be done one way, and one way only. Alex learned to eat green leaves from trees and to consume roots of flowers. He could not drink with his old friends because of the possible infection from germs. He even became fearful to breathe deeply because of the air contaminants.

The falcon had been watching the purification process over a period of time, feeling the loss of the time spent between old friends. One day he caught Alex in between classes, and he asked, "Alex, how have you been?"

Alex looked up with a tired smile. "My friend, I am so tired I could drop."

"I know I got you into this, but I don't want you to lose perspective on the world. Are you getting well?"

"I don't know," replied Alex. "I never thought I would be eating leaves and roots. I have never even heard of a wolf that has ever eaten leaves and roots like I have, but I am cooperative. With the preparations and careful procedures I go through each day, I rarely have time to do anything else. Do I look any better?"

The falcon did not know what to say. He had noticed some weight loss, but he did not know whether it would be good or bad to comment. Finally he said, "Frankly, Alex, I don't know what to think. It doesn't sound natural for a wolf to be eating like a deer."

"But, my friend, the latest study shows a low cancer rate in deer," responded Alex.

The falcon did not want to get into another argument with Alex, a more common occurrence lately. Finally he said, "Alex, I don't know which is worse: your internal confusion with your disease or your fight with the rest of the world. You are rejecting your friends, your home, your own natural place in the world. The world has always been a place of danger, and I am sure it may become more so. I even agree that food, air and water have to be respected for their impact on our health. But I am wondering if the fear of the cancer is not extending to your whole world. In other words, are you seeing your disease in everything around you?"

Alex could not answer his friend's questions. It was true that he had become sensitive to all the things that used to bring him joy, and now he questioned everything. In silence he walked away. He needed isolation and freedom in order to think things out. He was more confused than ever. His cancer had grown from a frog to ants to neuroses to sin to impurity. Now it encompassed the whole world.

Alex went to his favorite place for contemplation—a big, flat rock beside the tide pool by the ocean. The air was cool and clean, and it cleared his head. It was as if the mother of the sea talked and comforted him with the sounds of the waves, rocking his consciousness into other dimensions. He had come here many times to make decisions about life, and his altar was the rock.

Alex fell asleep almost immediately. His trip had taken most of his energy, and the warm sun relaxed his muscles quickly. He dreamed of J., only this time, as he approached the creature from across the meadow, the lines of identification were clearer. As he came within speaking distance, he could see that the creature's back was toward him. So as not to disturb him, Alex sat down and waited silently. Suddenly the creature turned and faced Alex, and the appearance stunned the great wolf. The creature was in the form of a dragon! He had big, green eyes and a wide mouth and huge teeth. His big body had what looked to be scales and horns, but although its overall appearance was frightening, Alex was not afraid. He was more infatuated and curious. He merely remained seated and observed the magic movements of the creature with an intense concentration.

"Alex, you are welcome," said the creature with a calm voice. "I am glad that you are not afraid of my form."

Alex thought for a moment. "Why a dragon? You have said many times before that you have several forms, yet now you come as a dragon. I know that I have never met a dragon before, only heard stories about them.

They are always portrayed as beasts of terror. Are you supposed to be terror?"

"Dragons were originally beasts of protection, protecting the homes and special altars of the past. Dragons represent power and mystery," replied the creature.

"Have I had a dragon before?" asked Alex.

"You have a dragon now, in your heart, to protect your life force. It has the dedication to safeguard your being through difficult times so that positive paths are taken."

"Does everyone have something as powerful as a dragon within them?" asked Alex.

"Something as powerful," responded the creature. It seemed that there would be more explanation, but he only smiled with his eyes.

Alex felt proud and honored, relishing the belief that a dragon would dwell within him. When he had taken the time to clarify that image for himself, he rose to ask another question, but the creature stopped his words with a gesture.

"You must continue your pilgrimage now," instructed the creature. "Awake and meet your next teacher."

Alex instantly awoke to meet the face of a dolphin.

The mystery of the body is great indeed,
With magnificent armies of cells,
An intelligence beyond mere human's thoughts,
A perfect orchestra of pure and clear tone.

Massive histories and evolutionary attunement
Have produced a magic harmony,
Yet humankind's true genius to date is the wisdom
Not to confront the challenge of disease alone.

Seven

The Dolphin

ALEX WAS A BIT STARTLED WHEN HE AWOKE TO FIND a dolphin's nose in his face. He slowly raised himself and addressed the dolphin in slow, deliberate tones. "Who are you?"

The dolphin's voice was kind. "I am Dr. G. I am here simply because I live in these waters. I'm sorry if I startled you."

"My name is Alex, and I come here often just to think and sort out issues in my life." Alex was unusually timid with his words and felt intimidated by the dolphin. He had always heard of the wisdom of dolphins but had never had a conversation with one before. This dolphin appeared to be a female, although he could not tell for sure.

"Yes, I know," responded the dolphin. "I have seen you here in the past, and I thought I would come meet you. But you seem troubled. You may want your privacy. Should I leave?"

"No, please stay. You used the name 'Doctor'. Maybe you could clear up some things for me."

"Yes, I will answer what I can."

Alex took a deep breath and slowly began his story. He knew the details would have to be specific, so he did not want to leave out anything. The dolphin was quiet and patient, listening with a warmth in her eyes and an implicit understanding of each step, each feeling and each explanation. Occasionally she made a supportive gesture or gave a questioning look, which reinforced Alex's storytelling. Although the dolphin did not discuss or actually dialogue with Alex, he could not remember a time when he felt more care and concern. He actually went so far in his mind to feel he was being loved by Dr. G.

Finally, at the end of the long description of his trek since the diagnosis, Alex blurted out, "I need to know what cancer is. I am almost afraid to ask it one more

time because I am frustrated with the confusion about the different answers. Please explain it to me so I can finally understand."

The dolphin said, "Yes, I can understand your anger as you attempt to comprehend and adjust to all the information you are processing, not only about what cancer is from a physical point of view but also what it means to your life. Let me, if you can, be with you for this time and help with the meaningfulness of this time. And, please, allow yourself to know that I come as a friend and as a teacher."

Alex nodded, feeling a great warmth sweep over his body.

The dolphin continued, "First, and most importantly, I would encourage you to relax. Stress is known to be a critical factor as a possible cause or at least a partner in all disease. Stress cuts down your immune system, your defense against disease, so that you have less capacity to fight disease. It is easier said than done to relax, especially when you are frightened. It is also possible that you have not learned a great deal about relaxation in our 'hurry-up' world. Let me teach you a simple approach.

"First, close your eyes and imagine yourself in a very relaxing place. Find the right one for you. Take a few minutes to find it and become very familiar with it. Become aware of the smells that would be there, the air, the feel of the temperature. If you could touch the earth where you are, do so in your mind's eye. If this is a place you have visited before, even as a pup, remember all the wonderful things about the place in as much detail as possible. Take several moments to dwell in this place. If there is an object, such as a rock or a leaf, that you could hold to help you concentrate, feel free to find it for this exercise."

Alex began to relax, imagining the spring of his second year. He recalled how carefree he felt, how free. He also began to realize the strain his body and mind had been under for a long time. He knew relaxation was vital.

The dolphin went on, "When you have found the imaginary place, begin to breathe very deeply, making sure that you breathe out as deeply as you breathe in. In fact, a very good technique is for you, or someone else, to count to seven each time you breathe in or out. For example, take a deep breath and breathe out as you count, '1...2...3...4...5...6...7'. Now breathe in as you count, '1...2...3...4...5...6...7'. Now begin to breathe out to the same count again and again. Continue to do this for ten minutes, remembering with each breath to relax and let go more and more each time. It may be hard to concentrate at first, but relaxation is a very important thing to learn."

Alex almost cried with relief from trying to deal with the complexity of his disease without the stress and fear of misunderstanding. All of a sudden, cancer was not so fearful. He felt himself willing to learn about himself without the threat of hearing a death sentence.

The dolphin was quiet for a time, and then continued, "There are some very important things to learn about cancer and what it is. Continue your breathing and relaxation while you are listening to this information. First of all, cancer cells exist in all of us throughout our lives in one way or another. They are cells that begin to grow in the wrong ways. Sometimes they grow like ants biting themselves and eventually killing themselves. Sometimes they grow like a seedless weed that withers quickly and dies away. Most of the time they grow without a source of nurturing, like a dinosaur without food, and they die away after a brief stay. All cancer cells are dumb and typically do themselves in by their very nature."

Alex opened his eyes and asked a question, "If we all have cancer naturally, what goes wrong that it kills us?"

The dolphin smiled and answered, "What causes cancer cells to grow in the first place? No one knows for sure, but more than likely they are caused by some trauma to the system, a virus, an infection, even bad food or water that creates tissue dysfunction. An injury or even being irritated over a long period of time, such as what happens to the lungs with the tar in cigarettes, will create strange cell formation. Even emotional distress taken to some extent can cause abnormal cell production. Any weakness in the body has the potential of poor cell formation, but as I have explained, by the nature of being abnormal, the environment in which they are born is not appropriate and they usually quickly dissolve."

"Now, before you ask why cancer becomes a life-threatening disease, I would ask you to relax to a deeper level, breathing deeply. Each time you breathe out, feel the tension leaving your body, and as the breath fills your body, also feel the nurturing of the universe come in. Take a moment to enjoy the relaxation of the present. You may want to visualize the abnormal cells in their natural state of confusion and inability to cope and survive under normal circumstances."

It was a good thing the dolphin went through the relaxation process because Alex had begun to get anxious about erroneous cancer cells parading through his body. He became fearful, but with the reminder to remain relaxed, he could concentrate on the information easier.

The dolphin shifted her position and continued, "Under abnormal circumstances, when the body's defenses are low, these abnormal cells are allowed to grow and multiply, until they finally become large enough to be recognized as bundles of tumors. The bundles are still vulnerable to dissolving, but because of the abnormal nature the body has not paid attention to it as an enemy.

"Now, the good new is that we have very effective, highly intelligent armies of defense. Let me describe some of the major divisions to you so that you can picture the magnificent system that has served you so well. Swimming around in your blood are millions of white blood cells called neutrophils, eosinophils and monocytes. These are what would be called the front line of defense and are extremely powerful. For example, neutrophils are the most plentiful and they can actually smell the enemy as it floats by the site where it is hiding. It immediately sticks to the wall of the enemy blood vessel, slithers through tiny openings of the wall, and locates the invader in split seconds. They sacrifice themselves by engulfing the enemies with poisons that kill the enemies along with the germs. In many ways they resemble the 'Marines' of the system.

"Neutrophils are plentiful and can reproduce within minutes. Imagine how thousands of these cells are always watchful in their sentry duty, protective of all gates and shores. They are your friends, as if a creative master mind leaves these wonderful creatures within your body to protect you."

Alex began to imagine strong wolf packs guarding the perimeter of his system. If an intruder were to appear, the wolves would collect around the enemy and destroy it.

The dolphin gave Alex some time to process the phase, and continued, "Monocytes are not as plentiful but a bit smarter. In fact, they are amazing. They are tireless stormtroopers who live in tissues and organs. Some wander throughout the entire system, patrolling

for trouble. When alerted to the enemy, they swell five to ten times their size and become the mighty *macro phages*, able to devour hundreds of invaders. They can squirt their enzymes into surrounding tissue and gobble what is left with insatiable appetites. What they can't destroy, they may imprison or preserve, encapsulated forever. They even have the capacity to fuse together to form giant cells and tackle the largest of any invader, or they can split apart to form armies of small attacking units."

In addition to his wolf packs, Alex imagined a group of whales, all his friends, swimming in his body, swallowing huge amounts of disease and enemy fishes, sifting out the good ones from the bad. He was thoroughly enjoying the triumph over evil.

Again, the dolphin waited, then continued, "One of the most interesting groups, as pertaining to abnormal cells such as cancer cells, is the white blood cells called lymphocytes. These cells usually wait in the lymphatic tissue—hence, the term 'lymphocytes'—and are transported through clear lymph fluid to attack hostile organisms. Unlike the gross attack by the neutrophils and macro phages, the lymphocyte has a memory for a particular foe and destroys it with the 'single-minded intensity of an assassin.' There are generally two types: a B-cell and a T-cell. Generally, the B-cell is the computer expert, who learns to designate bad guys from good guys. For example, when we get chicken pox or the measles as children, our B-cells learn their names and for the rest of our lives, anytime they enter our house they are recognized immediately and eliminated.

"T-cells could be considered the most highly trained of all, and they come under different names. There are the Killer T-cells, who have a way of infiltrating the cancer cells and exploding them. They work secretly and deadly with very high intelligence. Another T-cell is called the Helper-T, and it helps in the attack by adding fire power, like calling in the Air Force and Navy for the 'big bang.' A third kind of T-cell is the Suppressor T, the regulator who points out vulnerable areas to attack and can determine friend from foe when the smoke gets heavy—a radar expert. Before getting to the point of how you got the disease called cancer, let me also tell you about an amazing potion that these guys can mix up in order to actually burn holes in the armor of the cancer cells. This potion is called 'complement' and consists of

nine enzymes and is created by the immune system itself for any kind of invader."

For some reason Alex visualized the dragon of his dream sending out smaller dragons, all powerful in missionary strength and dedication. He began to feel a warm flow throughout his body, finding that as he relaxed he could concentrate more easily on the body's internal activity. For the first time in many days he felt a victory was at hand.

As if the dolphin were reading his mind, she said, "Now you are wondering how in the heck did you get a disease with all of these systems working for you. There are many possible answers and no one can give a specific response. The best guess is that there are many reasons to think that the immune system slows down from time to time, allowing diseases to catch on enough to give a fight. Stress and depression weaken the system greatly. For example, individuals get significantly more colds and flu when they are under the stresses of examinations. When people have marriage or work stress, they can quickly get sick. Also, immune systems respond to some foods and polluted air in negative ways. Radiation from the sun can create some lower immune functioning, which may explain skin cancer. I think over-indulgence of just about anything can affect your system in a bad way to create just enough letdown to allow disease to begin to grow.

"The good news is that your immune system is alive and capable of responding in full force. I can give you some ideas on what I know has been shown to enhance immunity functioning, but for the moment I would like you to just relax again with the imagery of what can be done within. As you breathe deeply and relax all your muscles, your body can release its stress and tension in order to begin to function at a higher level. Just as the athlete begins to prepare for an event by relaxing and concentrating on focusing the power of the body in a particular way, I would like for you to begin to breathe deeply and start visualizing the wonderful components of the immune system. Visualize the stormtroopers and Marines with all their courage and determination with a spiritual mission. Visualize the clever undercover agents with their extrasensory capacities that are gifts of a high-order intelligence, and the integrated teamwork of the T-cells who have one need: to be the heroes for you and to provide you with a proud regiment of happy forces of energy."

Alex was relaxed and confident as he asked, "If cancer clumps are what you say they are, why did the doctors treat me as they did?"

The dolphin smiled with her eyes as she explained, "Let me say something about the medical treatment you received. For cancer, medicine offers surgery, radiation and/or chemotherapy. Obviously, surgery intends for the removal of the cell bulk, making it easier for your body defenses to clean up the rest. Radiation treatment usually aims to kill off the cancer cells, and it may get a few good ones too but the expectation is that the normal balance can be re-established and the good cells will grow faster and stronger than the bad. Chemotherapy also kills off cells, large amounts of them, including good guys and bad guys. However, as I told you earlier, the good cells are made for your body and will bounce back. With this advantage, the system can manage the bad ones easier. The process was uncomfortable for you to experience, but you may think of it as a bath to wash everything clean so you can do it right. It is a great opportunity to rebuild the system with new and shiny parts."

Alex wanted to remain in his relaxed state as long as he could. He felt safe and comfortable, imagining the defenses that swam through his body. He also felt an understanding of what cancer was in his own terms. Gone were the frog and the ants. The fears about guilt and sin were gone, too.

Eventually Alex opened his eyes to see the dolphin smiling back at him. "Thank you," he said with a whisper.

The dolphin smiled and with a small flicker began a movement out to shore. "I will be back tomorrow," she called out.

Alex was sorry to see the dolphin leave, but he had so many things to tell his friend, the falcon. He ran to find him perched upon the branch of an oak, carrying on a conversation with some of his other friends. As Alex told of the dolphin's explanations, everyone became excited about the great wolf's enthusiasm. The group did not break until after the sun disappeared behind the horizon. Even after Alex was again alone with himself, he could not sleep, thinking of all the ramifications.

The next day, Alex waited for the dolphin from dawn. While he waited he practiced the relaxation techniques and reviewed every bit of information so that nothing would be wasted. He wanted to start exactly where they had left off.

Finally Dr. G. arrived, as warm as before. "Good morning," she said. "How was your night?"

"Wonderful. I am eager to learn more."

"Fine," the dolphin said as she got comfortable. "Did you dream at all?"

The question caught Alex off guard. Suspiciously, he remembered the eagle's interpretation of his dream as a symptom of neurosis. "Yes, but why do you want to know that?"

"Life is a dream. Without a dream we begin dying."

Alex reported all of his dreams of the creature, including the eagle's interpretation. To do so required a great amount of courage on Alex's part because these dreams had become very important to him.

The dolphin's response when Alex described the eagle was unexpected. She laughed and laughed. It was some time before she could regain her composure to explain herself to the stunned wolf.

"I'm sorry, Alex, but I find the eagle's interpretation amusing. It may even be true, but that would only lead you into the past. Your dreams are best understood in the future. They are our best compasses in our pilgrimages. The creature is a great gift. Listen to it as a source of love and wisdom."

"Love? What does that have to do with cancer?" asked Alex.

The dolphin took on a look of concern. "Love is what makes unmeaningful and confusing things understandable. For example, I have found sickness to be one of the few times in my life that I could really open up to those around me because I didn't have somewhere to go or someplace to be. Life became more real than ever before because of the way disease almost demands some genuine response to each situation. In fact, I sometimes think that God permits cancer as a renewal of priorities, a time to explore the path of meaningfulness. Cancer is not necessarily a death sentence. The fact is that there is no cancer that is totally terminal for everyone—many people *do* survive. Sure, cancer is a serious proposition and it will take tremendous efforts and soul searching to change its course. The risk is the same for a soldier going to a war. The struggle will be there, but it is a good bet that you will win. I guess the issue is the effort and reason behind the struggle.

"The body is a well-conditioned system. By that, I mean that its many parts respond as a whole to each and every thought you have. When you get sad, every cell in your body gets sad. When you get glad, every cell responds likewise. In order to obtain any goal, you have to put things in order."

Alex looked at the dolphin, trying to comprehend. "And love and dreams are what count?"

Patiently the dolphin explained, "Love is the positive energy that brings all other energy together. And love invests itself in dreams. 'Love' and 'dreams' are words that define what brings passion to your life and clarify the real priorities in your everyday experiences. In other words, Alex, you need to decide what your purpose and motives are, and allow your mind and body to integrate them."

"Put things in order," repeated Alex, trying to conceptualize the purpose in his life.

The dolphin changed her position as if she wanted to make the next point with extra energy. "I suppose what I mean by 'put things in order' is to put things into perspective, being honest about what is important and what is unimportant. Life is a decision. When we are young, our metabolism is so powerfully positive that energy for maintaining a powerful immune and protective system is effortless. As we get older and our natural energy is depleted, our overall strengths become day-to-day choices."

Alex thought about this for a long time, with the dolphin being quiet, waiting for the appropriate time to speak. For what seemed to be a long time, Alex looked at the dolphin with the most intense look in his eyes. He was almost breathless with desperation.

Finally he asked, "Dr. G., will I live?"

The dolphin asked in a soft way, "Before I answer that, I must ask you: Why do you want to live?"

The great wolf thought for a moment and immediately responded, "Well, I have a family who wants me around. I have things I must do. Of course, I have a thousand reasons to live—"

"No," interrupted the dolphin, "those are reasons not to die. Why do you want to live now?"

Alex was genuinely perplexed. Why did he want to live? He thought of the inconvenience of dying, the embarrassment of being sick, the fear of not knowing what death was. All of these were reasons for not dying, as the dolphin said.

The dolphin finally broke the silence. "I will be back tomorrow. Think about what we have said."

Alex was left with his thoughts and silence, with the sound of the ocean waves and sea gulls.

The next day Alex was waiting for the dolphin with excited anticipation. As soon as the dolphin was in sight, he danced with joy.

The dolphin smiled, "You seem to be in a different frame of mind today, Alex. You are anxious to tell me something."

"Yes, yes, yes," responded Alex. "I must tell you everything. I was troubled by your question yesterday, and I stewed on it all day and partly through the night. It was as if my whole life meant nothing until I discovered the answer. I could not take another step, breathe another breath. Finally I fell asleep and had this magnificent dream. I dreamt of the creature again, and I asked him the question, 'Why do I want to live?' He did not answer in words, but suddenly he began to laugh. And as he laughed, music began to play. As the music became louder and louder, he began to dance. He danced and sang and laughed. He danced with me. He danced with other beings. I began to laugh and dance and sing. I forgot the question until I awoke, still dancing and singing. The dream made no sense other than a relief from my heavy thinking. Then just as I began to describe the dream to my friend, the falcon, it all made sense."

"It is the dance, the dance of life that I want to live! Don't you see what I mean, I want to learn a new dance, a new song. To live means to understand the joys of being and dancing."

The dolphin smiled, "To dance is to live."

"Is this what is known as healing?" asked Alex.

The dolphin said, "I would like to define healing in a way that goes beyond the concept of tissue binding and killing germs. To heal is to become *whole*. To heal is to bring mercy and awareness to ourselves in every facet, and to learn to be what we are or perhaps to change to sing a new song or to live a new dream. We have learned to be many of our ways, yet we do not want to be those ways and we use up so much energy attempting to make them right. It is no wonder we fatigue and run out of energy. Our cells know and respond as we think. After a long while of living in our same rut with all of its nightmares, we begin to feel hopeless and helpless. To heal means to meet ourselves in a new way, becoming whole in the sense of reclaiming the interests and dreams in an active way, perhaps to renew who we think we are to ourselves.

"This awakening of energies is often not easy. In fact, it may be painful because it also awakens the hurts and sufferings of our lives. Awakening may not happen for survival either. Sometimes tissue is already so destroyed that life quality is to the point where continuing life for the sake of one's ego is unproductive to one's development. Sometimes it is time to surrender to the demands of time so that you can focus upon a more important part of your life."

Alex asked, "Dr. G., why did I get cancer, and not others? Am I the kind of person who gets it and not others? Why am I the unlucky one?"

The dolphin said with a warm voice, "My friend, you ask the same question I hear most from patients with cancer—not what caused the disease, but why? Why me? Why now? Why here? It appears that the meaningfulness of the event is the most important thing to know. Sometimes people conclude that it is God's punishment for some sin in life. Other individuals have decided that cancer is a personal flaw in their lives or personalities and count it as an embarrassment. Sometimes there is a kind of guilt that this should not have happened to me because I should have been smarter or should have thought better thoughts. On the other hand, many patients have considered the disease a just and appropriate consequence to a lifestyle or belief system. Often I hear, 'I should have expected it because I have never had a proper life anyway.' Many times people attempt to strike a bargain, believing that if they change their lives they will receive a longer life.

"The question that finally emerges is: How can we use all that is given as a means of stepping further into love for ourselves and others, including our disease and our emotions about our disease? Cancer is one of the most threatening to us because it means a definite change in ourselves, a possible surgical removal of a body part, a loss of some function, a lifestyle adaptation, a loss of a relationship, or even our inevitable death. All that is dear to us is threatened, and we come face-to-face with all of our values and concepts. We also realize the insignificance of our material possessions. We are naked to this disease, and being naked is extremely frightening. But nakedness can also be freedom, without the restraint of masks or pretension."

Alex said, "I don't like the demand for change. I like to take things when I want, in my own time."

The dolphin laughed. "We have little choice but to face the challenge and find our true dreams. In taking the path of wholeness, previous conflicts can be seen as rich and fertile ground for insight into causes of suffering, and this self-awareness can allow us to move beyond suffering. When we cross the bridge from fear to opportunity and when we go beyond our blocks of needless self-destruction and self-hatred, then the question of 'Why' disappears. What becomes important is the possibility of dancing a new dance and singing a new song without fear.

"An analogy that comes to mind is a person who has saved money a whole lifetime in case of emergency. Throughout life there was always a sacrifice for this possible event. As the funds grew and grew, a paranoia arose that perhaps someone would take the money away

and leave this person vulnerable to ruin. Further
concerns made matters even worse, like the government
looking unstable or inflation. After a diagnosis of
cancer, all of this did not matter. There was no need for
hiding, no need for fears, no need for isolation, no
concern for earthly matters, no concern for governments
or problems. Finally, this person reaches a time in life
that provides for true exploration of life without the
chains of mythical ties to life and happiness."

"You make it sound as if we should be glad to have
disease," said Alex.

Ignoring the cynical tone, the dolphin looked into
Alex's eyes with sincerity. "Alex, disease is often a brutal
and terrifying experience, but it is not an enemy. It is a
teacher. It is part of you for a reason. Yes, sometimes
disease can be your greatest challenge to be your greatest
self. How fortunate we are when we are given the
opportunity and time to let go of our defenses with love
in our hearts. How sad it must be not to have time to
process our thoughts without the sense of rushing and
immediacy. Perhaps your white blood cells need to
dance a new tune as well as you. Perhaps your
self-concept needs renewal.

"Friend, please know that the pilgrimage is what
makes you and me alike. Everyone, regardless of race,
creed or class, is connected to this pilgrimage. Rather
than feeling alone, feel free to know that I am unafraid
to be with you and share what I know, and to hear what
you know and experience. I know of no easy answers to
our existences, but I do know that love is the only reality
that remains constant in life. Even our white blood cells

love each other; otherwise, they would have decided not to be with you long ago."

The dolphin turned to go. "I will be gone for a while, but I want to assure you that cancer does not take away your freedom of will. Cancer does not restrict you to being a submissive person with no choices; rather, it gives you new alternatives. As I said before, cancer is not always terminal. There are people who have been diagnosed with every kind of cancer and continued to live normal lives. True, it is a serious process that calls for your total attention and thought. Your white blood cells can be called on for their power in cancer cell control, but they are creatures of habit and have been responding to specific signals all of your life. It will take a great deal of effort and understanding to find out what signals relate to their actions. It may take a new lifestyle, new relationships, a new approach to life. Whatever your decisions, I want you to know that you are surrounded by love and, although the journey may appear frightening, you will find that most of the fears are centered in our own myths and 'boogiemen.' We make life much too complicated than it really is. I believe that to really understand this process, we must think like children. To a child, love is understood simply as caring. The world is enormous, but we can are grounded based upon our sense of community with all living beings."

Alex watched the dolphin swim out of sight, not feeling alone anymore. He was alive and he had a whole community within himself who loved him. He would live.

As beautiful as the body can be,
It is still part of the animal.
The other part that kins us with the angels
Is the vital self, the soul.

Lest we forget, we are always more than we see,
Greater than pain, greater than stress, than even demons.
We are the world, the stars, the universe,
As long as to fear the self is never sold.

Eight

Healing

"WHAT ARE YOU DOING?" INQUIRED THE FALCON. HE had been observing Alex for the last fifteen minutes from his perch in a tree. Alex was sitting with his eyes closed and breathing very deeply. The falcon was curious, but he had waited patiently for his friend to emerge from his quiet state. Finally, however, he decided to break the silence.

"Just concentrating on listening to my body," Alex answered without opening his eyes.

"Oh, I'm sorry. I will come back when you are finished," said the falcon with an apologetic tone.

"No, I can only concentrate for so long, then my mind begins to wander," Alex said as he opened his eyes with a smile. "Besides, I have been wanting to see you. I haven't seen you in the last few days."

"I have been preparing for our trip to the south. Along about this time, when the wind begins to shift and the chill gets into the air, we usually move our nests to seek warmer temperatures. You remember how we do it, Alex. In fact, one summer you helped us move."

"Yes, I remember, but I did not realize it was that time. I am perceiving time differently this year."

"Oh yes, how are you doing with all of that information the dolphin gave you? Are you going back for treatment?"

"Yes, I am going back. In fact, I am going back to all of the doctors. I have come to recognize that there is truth in all the different approaches to healthcare. The specialists I have seen represent different metaphors for the same process. I am on a learning quest."

"All of them!" asked the falcon. He was surprised and puzzled. "I thought you were turned off by the whole bunch, especially the eagle."

"Yes, but I was mistaking the message with the messenger. They all meant well. I have to decide for myself what is good information, but I still regard them as my teachers. Like all teachers they get carried away with themselves from time to time, but if I listen with my heart instead of with my ego, I find amazing treasures for myself."

"You do seem more relaxed and happy," observed the falcon. He was genuinely pleased with his friend since Alex's conversations with the dolphin, but he also was curious about the direction of the great wolf's life. He could always predict Alex's behavior before, primarily because of his compulsive approach to life, always weighing consequences and using methodical steps.

This had kept him from getting killed many times. But lately Alex had exhibited a much more relaxed and care-free attitude.

"The dolphin was right about changing my life." Alex broke into the falcon's thoughts. "I have learned some of the most important things in my life. For example, I have always been a being who was responsible for other beings. My father was killed when I was a cub, and being the oldest, I had to take care of everyone. I didn't mind. In fact, I took a lot of pride in being able to handle it. I took care of my mother, my sisters and brothers, as well as my own family later. I was very good at being the 'do-er' but was not good at being a receiver of the doings. In fact, I partly resented acts of kindness toward me. Now I have learned that the definition of love is both giving and receiving, and I am now allowing myself to accept love. Boy! It is hard, but it has made a big difference in my relationships with my family. And you know what? They say that for the first time they like me, really like me. All the time before they had always felt rejected when I would not allow their help. Can you believe that? And all this time I thought I was being so strong and brave. It is a new world for me."

The falcon could hardly believe it. The great wolf was describing what the falcon had observed for many years; he had often wished that Alex could receive a well-deserved thanks and praise for his efforts. The falcon was silent with these thoughts but nodded agreement with each statement. He wanted to sing and praise his friend, but he certainly did not want to make light of Alex's valuable discovery.

"But the dolphin was wrong about one thing," Alex continued. "Cancer is a friend in the sense that it forced me to think about my life, but it is also an enemy to be dealt with, to be overcome by all of my forces at hand. I guess if it was not so deadly I would not have focused upon it, but by being the worst foe I have faced, I am challenged to be my very best."

"But Alex, what is your best? You have always been a great wolf. I am not sure what best would be."

Alex's eyes glistened as he spoke. "I can be the best loving being I can be. I can live the best life I can. I can marvel at the mysteries of life and better understand the best relationships to be known. Better yet, I can come to know the best dream I have."

He continued, "Life is a dream, like the creature in my dream said. If you don't have a dream to focus on, you are dying. It has to be bigger than you are so that you have to put things in perspective to achieve it, but it has to be small enough to be your own."

The falcon hated to ask this question, but it was out of him before he knew it. "Does that mean that you will not die?"

Alex thought for a few moments, then slowly spoke. "It does not make any difference. Death will meet all of us, eventually, face-to-face, in some form. Whether it is heart disease, worms, or cancer, it is dictated by the lessons to be learned. Death is not the teacher, only the transition. Whether or not I win this time is not as important as the style and character with which I learn from the experience. Make no mistake about my intent. I am playing with all the energy I have to win, but only in taking myself to the brink can I know myself in the best way."

The falcon listened, understanding as much as he could. "Are you depressed?"

"Depressed? A little because I have to realize that I have to change my life. I confess that I have some fear about not knowing exactly how my life is going to change, but I am mostly excited. The dolphin said that a lot of the excess mental baggage would not have to be there anymore, like worrying about what is going to happen next year or ten years from now. I am focusing on me now, and I can appreciate things now. I had always worried about what was going to happen, or what had happened. I am amazed to discover that so many wonderful things are happening right now. I can enjoy life much more, like watching that bee over there or smelling the aroma from the flower there, or having the pleasure of your company right now."

The falcon was surprised by his own awareness of pleasure in the genuineness of the conversation. He knew that Alex had always been forthright, but this was almost an honor to have him share such deep and intimate thoughts. But the falcon was also a realistic thinker. "Not all things are beautiful, Alex. Are you saying that all can be pleasurable and lovely? Are you going to deny the horrible things like hunger and hate?"

"No, these are even more horrible when we live from moment to moment, because we are more aware of the feelings. But we also recognize that many things are not as horrible as we thought, because we tend to make things worse than they are. It is not horrible to miss an appointment, as I once thought it was. It is not horrible to be rejected. It is uncomfortable, but not horrible. It is not horrible to die. It is challenging, but it has always been challenging, from the first breath we take. It is the hopelessness and lack of resources that we fear as horrible."

Both the falcon and the wolf fell into silence. It was not that they had nothing to say. It was a time of reverence for each other and a peace between them. There was a bond of love. The healing had begun.

Epilogue

Lifesong

*Embrace life with both arms and mind
outstretched. Enter into it fully and lovingly, and
with the distinct sense that the finest adventure,
adventure unlike any other in history, adventure
that could not happen to another being alive
awaits you day after day. And as you approach
your last days, you will face them, too, with great
and heightened expectation of a lover awaiting her
beloved.*

*As you move through your years, through each
small movement in time, touch its grand and
intricate textures, feel the fluttering it causes in
the universe of all being. Let no encounter, no*

dream escape your knowing heart. For nothing, no matter how small or silly, is banal. All is sacred—all is created from the same splendid fabric that birthed the wisest and most holy among us all.

Know that the everlasting—and what being here in the body, in this place, is really about—is almost always invisible. It is the quiet impulse, smothered by convention and authority. The longings silenced by necessity. Reality, the reality of what is real and enduring, lies in the hidden naked spaces of feeling, in the instant of divine recognition that there is absolutely no separation between you and any other act of creation. This moment of recognition of the connection of all that was and is and will be is the definition and purpose of true healing.

Only a deep and intense concentration wrought by meditation or suffering lets the inner voice, long silent, shine through the cacophony and confusion and materialism of the world. Listen carefully to the voice that is you. Cherish it. Nurture it with your love and let it sing. It is no easy task, mind you, singing in a voice gone rusty from a lifetime of disuse is far more risky than silently searching for the messages from your inner being.

*The battle for emotional survival that you fought
as a child, a young adult, or whatever age you
encountered the dragon that challenged the
exquisite balance of your sanity, will never have to
be waged again, against any adversary, as long as
you live. Each subsequent encounter will be
diminished in its intensity; each foe will be
recognized and named and defused long before the
damage to the inviolate core that is you can be
touched by its unmerciful fangs. And you will
grow and flourish from the knowledge of your
strength.*

*Passion and creativity are the sustenance of
eternal life in this world. No matter how wicked,
no matter how profane. Any soul, sparked by the
insatiable twins of embellished consciousness, can
live forever. When they wane—as they
must—diminished by pain and the pure
unadulterated fatigue of having made too many
changes, then life will move on to its next and
finest dimension.*

— Dr. Jeanne Achterberg

More Resources for Healing and Recovery

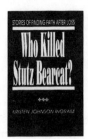

WHO KILLED STUTZ BEARCAT?
Stories of Finding Faith after Loss

Kristen Johnson Ingram

Paper, $8.95, 0-89390-264-0

Nine stories encourage readers to find courage within themselves after facing losses. Reflection questions will lead readers beyond the author's stories and into their own. As readers reflect upon personal experiences, they may discover their own possibilities for resurrection. This book is appropriate for grief ministry work, pastoral counseling, initiation groups, or individual reflection.

PARTNERS IN HEALING
Redistributing Power in the Counselor-Client Relationship

Barbara Friedman, PhD

Paper, $14.95, 0-89390-226-8

The traditional therapy model requires one person to have power over another. That's trouble, says Dr. Barbara Friedman, herself a practicing psychologist. With this book, she proposes a therapeutic model in which counselor and client interact as equal partners in the healing process. This unique book is must reading for therapists, clergy and pastoral counselors, lay counselors, and clients.

HEALING OUR LOSSES
A Journal for Working Through Your Grief

Jack Miller, PhD

Paper, $10.95, 0-89390-255-1

The author shares experiences of loss in his own life and guides you to record memories, thoughts, and feelings about loss in your life. This book offers comfort to anyone grieving a loss and can help eventually heal the pain. The process may be used by an individual or in a group setting.

Improve Your Storytelling Skills!

STORYTELLING STEP-BY-STEP

Marsh Cassady, PhD

Paper, $9.95
0-89390-183-0

Marsh Cassady, a storytelling and drama instructor, takes you through all the steps of storytelling: selecting the right story for your audience, adapting your story for different occasions, analyzing it to determine the best way to present it, preparing your audience, and presenting the story. Includes many story examples.

CREATING STORIES FOR STORYTELLING

Marsh Cassady, PhD

Paper, $9.95
0-89390-205-5

This book picks up where the author's popular *Storytelling Step-by-Step* leaves off. Find out how to get ideas to create your own original stories, adapt stories to different audiences, plot a story, create tension, and write dialogue.

Order Form

Order these resources from your local bookstore, or mail this form to:

QTY	TITLE	PRICE	TOTAL

Subtotal: _____

CA residents add 7¼% sales tax
(Santa Clara Co. residents, 8¼%): _____

Postage and handling
($2 for order to $20; 10% of order over $20 but less than $150; $15 for order of $150 or more): _____

Total: _____

Resource Publications, Inc.
160 E. Virginia Street #290 - B7
San Jose, CA 95112-5876
(408) 286-8505
(408) 287-8748 FAX

☐ My check or money order is enclosed.
☐ Charge my ☐ VISA ☐ MC.

Expiration Date _____

Card # _____ - _____ - _____ - _____

Signature _____

Name (print) _____

Institution _____

Street _____

City/State/ZIP _____